WONDER WOMEN

CARLTON
BOOKS

THIS IS A CARLTON BOOK

Published in 2019 by Carlton Books Limited,
an imprint of the Carlton Publishing Group,
20 Mortimer Street, London W1T 3JW

ISBN: 978-1-78312-475-6

Text, design and illustration copyright © 2019 Carlton Books Limited

Cover design by Deborah Vickers

All rights reserved. This book is sold subject to the condition that it may not be reproduced, stored in a retrieval system or transmitted in any form or by any means, electronic, mechanical, photocopying, recording or otherwise, without the publisher's prior consent.

A catalogue record for this book is available from the British Library.

10 9 8 7 6 5 4 3 2 1

Printed in China

THE ILLUSTRATORS

Andrew Archer
Andrew worked in the industry for a few years only to realize 80 per cent of his "design" was actually illustration, so he became an illustrator. He didn't take art at school but he did eat crayons which quite possibly is where his off-beat colour palettes come from!

Kelly Thompson
After an initial career in fashion photography, Kelly began to capture her subjects as ephemeral illustrations. As a freelance artist, Kelly first works by hand, sketching up in pencil, before using Photoshop and adding colour with help from her trusty Wacom.

Anna Higgie
Anna is an Australian-born illustrator now living and working in Bristol. She spends most of her time in her Stokes Croft studio where she uses a combination of traditional and digital techniques to create her illustrations.

Pietari Posti
Finnish-born illustrator Pietari moved to sunny Barcelona to set up his own studio. He is greatly inspired by nature and loves trying out new illustration techniques. His bold shapes and expressive style have attracted a diverse range of international clients.

Jessica Singh
Jessica is from Australia and a graduate of Central Saint Martins in London. Inspired by her Indian heritage, she loves vibrant colour and traditional textile designs. When she's not drawing, Jessica loves travelling, walking in nature or collecting crystals.

Sofia Bonati
Born in Argentina, Sofia now lives in the UK. She first studied geology before completing a degree in graphic design and illustration. To her soft pencil drawings, she likes to add inks, watercolour, and gouache – making her female portraits elegant and refined.

Jonny Wan
Jonny was born in Sheffield but now lives and works in Manchester. Failure to grow beyond 5'7" saw his dreams of a multi-million dollar salary playing basketball dashed and he decided to pursue the next best thing – illustration!

Susan Burghart
Susan is an American-born illustrator based in the UK. Heavily influenced by her graphic design background, she also loves typography. She works primarily in digital and likes experimenting with collage and screen printing.

WONDER WOMEN

TRUE STORIES OF

ICONIC WOMEN

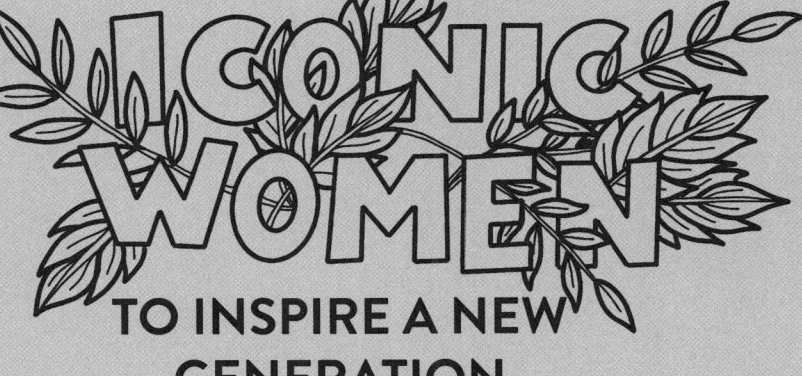

TO INSPIRE A NEW GENERATION

CONTENTS

05
INTRODUCTION

06
CLEOPATRA

10
JOAN OF ARC

14
ADA LOVELACE

18
HARRIET TUBMAN

22
MARIE CURIE

26
AMELIA EARHART

30
FRIDA KAHLO

34
ROSA PARKS

38
DR JANE GOODALL

42
VALENTINA TERESHKOVA

46
JUNKO TABEI

50
ZAHA HADID

54
MICHELLE OBAMA

58
MALALA YOUSAFZAI

62
TIMELINE

64
INDEX

INTRODUCTION

Inside this book, you'll find the totally awesome **true stories** of **14 women** who changed the world in different ways!

Meet **Valentina Tereshkova**, the first woman in space. There's **Junko Tabei**, who conquered the world's highest mountains. **Joan of Arc**'s speciality was leading armies (and busting stereotypes). **Rosa Parks** kick-started events that ended segregation in the USA. And then there's **Frida Kahlo**, the artist who was the inspiration for this book.

Not all the women in this book lived a gazillion years ago. Some lived much more recently. Others are still alive today. Some are famous. Some, not famous enough.

But whether a computer whizzkid, a scientist, an aviator, a leader, a painter, a lawyer, an astronaut, an architect, a mountaineer, a political activist, an architect or a conservationist, these women all have one thing in common. They're **feminists**, which means they believe that men and women are equal. (Which they are. Obviously.) And they've refused to leave it up to men to make history.

You might know what you want to be when you grow up. You might not. If not, this book might give you a few ideas. But we not-so-secretly hope that it'll inspire you too.

Now turn the page, start reading...
and then change the world.

CLEOPATRA

EGYPTIAN ICON

Cleopatra's life was a rollercoaster of love, war and tragedy. She was the last pharaoh of Ancient Egypt and one of history's biggest celebrities. Her looks were legendary and she loved to make an entrance, once appearing on a golden barge with purple sails and silver oars. But she had to be tough and ruthless too if she wanted to stay in control of Egypt and stop the Romans invading…

> "I will not be triumphed over."
>
> Cleopatra

NAME: **Cleopatra VII Thea Philopator**
BORN: **about 69 BCE**
DIED: **12 August, 30 BCE**
NATIONALITY: *Egyptian*
PROFESSION: *Ruler*

Cleopatra thought she was a living goddess and is said to have looked *fabulous*. But her famous beauty often outshines the fact that she was also highly educated, very clever and a brilliant leader. Even though her family was Greek, she spoke Egyptian and followed Egypt's customs, which made her super popular too. Under her rule, the country boomed.

Cleopatra fell in love with not one, but two of the greatest Roman leaders ever. First, there was Julius Caesar. When he was killed, Cleopatra joined forces with Marc Antony. Together, they fought against Caesar's adopted son – Octavian – who wanted to rule Rome *and* take over Egypt. Their luck ran out when Octavian won. To avoid capture, Cleopatra and Marc Antony both killed themselves. Their tragic story is retold in a play by William Shakespeare called *Antony and Cleopatra*.

JOAN OF ARC
TEEN LEADER

Joan of Arc believed that God wanted her to banish the English from France. At first, she was astonished. She was a teenage girl, not a great soldier. How could she lead an army into battle? Yet she could. And she did. Joan of Arc showed that it wasn't just men who could be heroes.

NAME: **Jeanne d'Arc**

BORN: **about 1412**

DIED: **30 May, 1431**

NATIONALITY: **French**

PROFESSION: **Military leader**

Joan of Arc was 13 years old when she had her first vision. God wanted her to gather an army to help fight the English. She didn't know what to think. But the visions went on and on until she obeyed. She cut her hair short, dressed in men's clothes and went to see Charles VII.

At first, the French king thought the idea of a teenage girl leading his army was ridiculous. But then he wondered if Joan really could win. So he decided to let her try. And, armed with a flag instead of a weapon, she led the French into battle… and to victory.

A year later, Joan of Arc was captured by the English and burned at the stake, aged just 19. Nearly five hundred years later, she was made a saint. She is now the patron saint of soldiers and France.

> "I am not afraid; I was born to do this."

Joan of Arc

ADA LOVELACE
COMPUTER WHIZZKID

Ada Lovelace's father was a poet – a very famous one, called Lord Byron. But her mother was a mathematician. And it was Lady Byron who decided exactly what her daughter would study: maths and science. It was a great decision for computer science. Ada would use her knowledge to help develop one of the most important inventions ever.

> "Understand well as I may, my comprehension can only be an infinitesimal fraction of all I want to understand."

Ada Lovelace

NAME: **Augusta Ada King-Noel, Countess of Lovelace**

BORN: **10 December, 1815**

DIED: **27 November, 1852**

NATIONALITY: **British**

PROFESSION: **Mathematician and computer scientist**

Ada Lovelace was lucky. In the nineteenth century, many people thought that some subjects were so tricky only boys were clever enough to understand them. But not Lady Byron. She hired a private tutor to make sure that her daughter was given an excellent education that included maths and science. The incredible thing was that Ada didn't just love these subjects – she was brilliant at them too.

When she was 17, Ada met Charles Babbage. The genius mathematician had designed the difference engine – the first calculator ever – and showed her how it worked. She was amazed. Next, Babbage designed the analytical engine – the world's first computer. When he asked her help to translate a French article about the analytical engine into English, she went one better. Ada also added her own ideas for how the analytical engine could be programmed. Now, she is known as the world's first computer programmer.

HARRIET TUBMAN
FREEDOM CHAMPION

Harriet Tubman was born into slavery; her life was tougher than you can ever imagine. But she was *determined* to escape. Once she did, she risked her life to help others escape too. During her long, long life, she campaigned for the end of slavery and for black people's rights. She is now an American icon.

> *Every great dream begins with a dreamer. Always remember, you have within you the strength, the patience, and the passion to reach for the stars to change the world.*

Harriet Tubman

NAME: **Araminta Ross (later changed to Harriet Tubman)**

BORN: **around 1820**

DIED: **10 March 1913**

NATIONALITY: **American**

PROFESSION: **Civil rights activist**

No one knows Harriet Tubman's date of birth, because slave owners didn't keep records. She, her parents and eight brothers and sisters were all slaves who lived on a large plantation in Maryland. The work was tough; they were fed little and beaten often. At last, Harriet decided to run away. And on the night of 17 September 1849, she did.

On the way north, she looked out for secret signals left by those who wanted to help runaway slaves. The route she followed became known as the Underground Railroad. Finally, she reached Philadelphia – she was free! But her family wasn't, so she went back to rescue them. Harriet returned again and again to guide hundreds of slaves to freedom. She was never caught. And neither were any of the slaves she helped to escape.

MARIE CURIE

FAB PHYSICIST

Marie Curie was a Nobel Prize-winning physicist and chemist. But her science superstardom didn't come easily. First she fought to be able to study science at all. Then she spent years carrying out research in an old shed. But her hard work paid off. And thank goodness it did.

NAME: **Maria Skłodowska Curie**

BORN: **7 November 1867**

DIED: **4 July 1934**

NATIONALITY: **Polish-French**

PROFESSION: **Scientist**

When Marie grew up in Poland, science in schools was banned. So her father taught his children at home instead. Marie was a top student and after studying in secret, she went to the Sorbonne – a famous university in Paris. It was here that Marie met Pierre Curie, a physics professor. They married and went on to become one of the greatest double acts in the history of science.

When the Curies learned that Henri Becquerel had discovered radioactivity, they were curious. Perhaps they could find out more. After years of hard work, they found the chemical elements polonium and radium. These could help treat cancer. Marie and Pierre Curie and Henri Becquerel were awarded the Nobel Prize for Physics in 1903. She was the first woman ever to receive one. And in 1911, she was awarded the Nobel Prize for Chemistry too.

> *Life is not easy for any of us. But what of that. We must have perseverance and above all confidence in ourselves. We must believe that we are gifted for something ...*

Marie Curie

AMELIA EARHART
PIONEER PILOT

Amelia Earhart is famous for being the first woman to fly across the Atlantic Ocean. But she did more than that. She also inspired women to think about doing all sorts of careers – even those that had always been done by men. And by being such an amazing pilot, she showed everyone that the sky really was the limit!

NAME: Amelia Mary Earhart

BORN: 24 July 1897

DISAPPEARED: 2 July 1937

NATIONALITY: American

PROFESSION: Pilot

Just because people told Amelia Earhart that engineering, film directing and law weren't for girls didn't mean that she agreed with them. Quite the opposite. She actually kept a scrapbook of women who were great at these jobs. Meanwhile, *she* wanted to be a pilot.

She learnt to fly, saved enough money to buy her own plane and then decided to break records, just like men. First, she became the first woman to fly to a height of 4,267 metres. Next, she became the first woman to fly across the Atlantic. From then on, records tumbled, one after another, until the Big One. Could she fly around the world? Amelia Earhart was going to give it a good try. She set off on 1 June 1937… but she never made it. However, the world has never forgotten that she tried.

"*Women must try to do things as men have tried. When they fail, their failure must be but a challenge to others.*"

Amelia Earhart

FRIDA KAHLO

REBEL ARTIST

Frida Kahlo is famous for many things. She's famous for her artwork, especially her fabulous self-portraits. She's famous for standing up for her communist beliefs. But perhaps she is most famous for refusing to act as everyone expected a woman to act. She did what she wanted to do. And she described her amazing life story using art.

"The only thing I know is that I paint because I need to, and I paint whatever passes through my head..."

Frida Kahlo

NAME: **Magdalena Carmen Frida Kahlo y Calderón**

BORN: **6 July 1907**

DIED: **13 July 1954**

NATIONALITY: **Mexican**

PROFESSION: **Artist**

Frida never expected to be an artist. She wanted to be a doctor. But when she was 18, she suffered terrible injuries in a bus crash, which put an end to her studies. After the accident, Frida spent months recovering. Stuck in a plaster cast, she began to do something she'd always loved. She began to paint. At long last, she began to recover and then to walk again.

Frida's paintings are easy to recognise. Their bright, symbolic style showed her Mexican culture. Her colours held meaning too. For her, green stood for sadness and science. Yellow meant madness, sickness, fear and joy. Many of her paintings were self-portraits that showed her pain. Her art is said to be surreal – this is when things are mixed together in a strange, dreamlike way.

Now, Frida is one of the most famous artists in the world.

> "I would like to be remembered as a person who wanted to be free... so other people would be also free."

Rosa Parks

ROSA PARKS

CIVIL RIGHTS STAR

When Rosa Parks was born, parts of the USA were segregated. This meant that black and white people did many everyday things apart from each other. There were separate schools, separate swimming pools, separate toilets and even separate water fountains. Rosa hated it. But surely not even she could have dreamt that her simple act of bravery would change *everything*...

NAME: **Rosa Louise McCauley Parks**

BORN: **4 February 1913**

DIED: **24 October 2005**

NATIONALITY: **American**

PROFESSION: **Civil rights activist**

Rosa had been made to feel that she wasn't as good as a white person for her whole life. By the time she was 42, she'd had enough. On 1 December 1955, when she was travelling on a bus in Montgomery, Alabama, she fought back. That day, the bus driver asked Rosa to stand so that a white man could sit in her seat. Rosa didn't move. The police were called, she was arrested and she was fined. She refused to pay, telling them that the fine was illegal. Others agreed. They decided not travel on Montgomery's buses until the law was changed.

After 381 days, the US Supreme Court ruled against Montgomery's segregation law. The protesters had won! Now, everyone could sit wherever they wanted. Even better, the Civil Rights Act of 1964 meant that anyone could use any public facility. All because of Rosa.

37

DR JANE GOODALL

CHAMPION OF CHIMPS

Jane Goodall is a total chimp expert. She has spent over half a century patiently watching how they live, behave and communicate with each other. She also supports the conservation of animals and the environment too. She was rewarded for a lifetime of achievements when she was made Dame Jane Goodall in 2003.

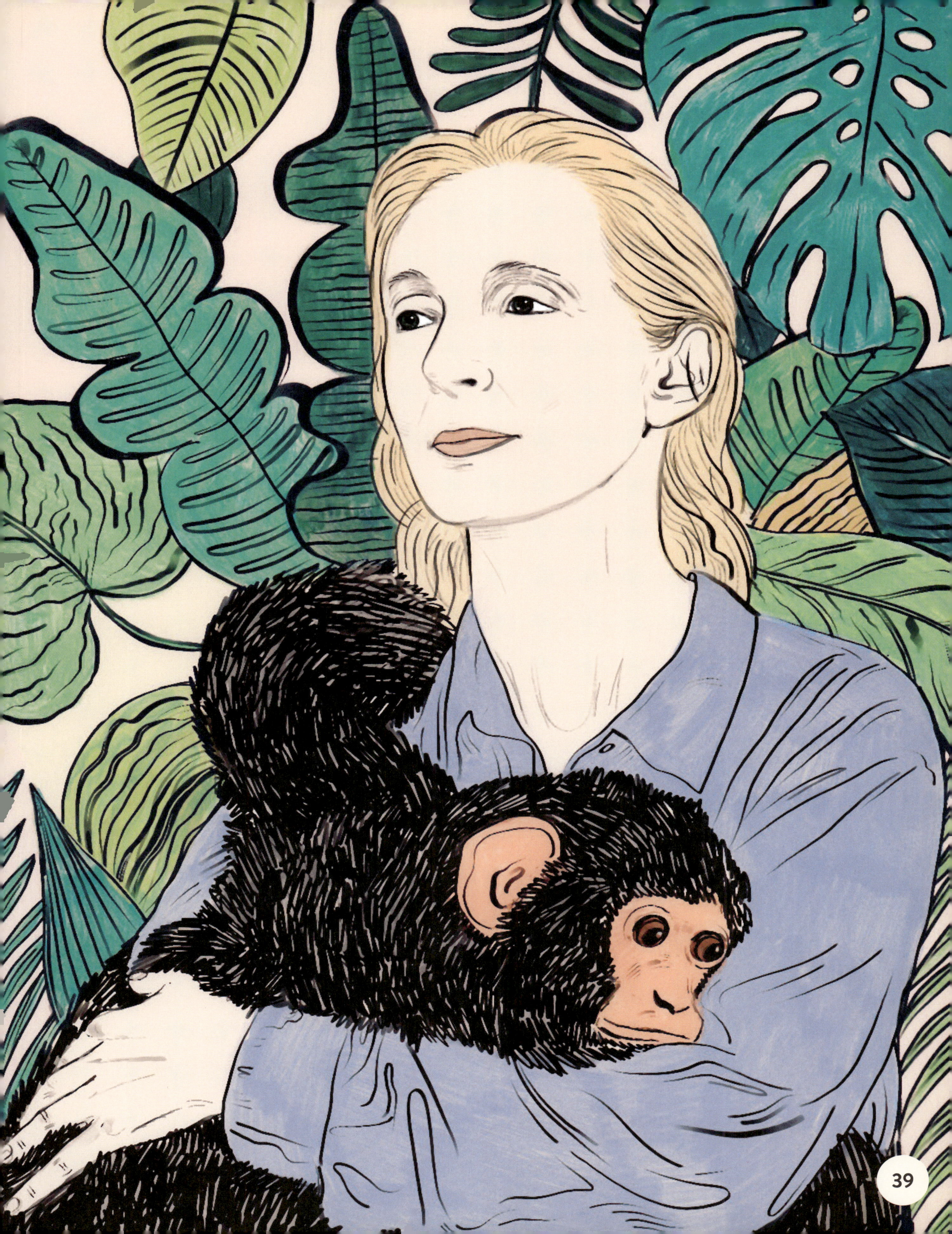

NAME: **Valerie Jane Morris-Goodall**

BORN: **3 April 1934**

NATIONALITY: **British**

PROFESSION: **Chimpanzee expert and conservationist**

Jane Goodall has been super interested in animal behaviour ever since she was very young. But in England, there weren't many exotic animals. For that, she'd have to travel abroad. So when she was old enough, Jane went to Tanzania in Africa. There, she got the perfect job – as a chimpanzee researcher!

One day, Jane watched a chimp make a spoon from a twig, then dip it into a termite nest to scoop up insects. This was a huge discovery. It had always been thought that humans were the only species to make and use tools. The news would change the way people looked at chimps *and* humans. She carried on her work for over half a century. Meanwhile, she set up the Jane Goodall Institute, to "improve the lives of people, animals and the environment". She also founded Roots and Shoots, a community action programme which aims to make the world a better place.

"The least I can do is speak out for those who cannot speak for themselves."

Jane Goodall

VALENTINA TERESHKOVA

ROCKET WOMAN

Human spaceflight is a pretty awesome thing. Since 1961, only a few hundred people have done it. Yet Valentina Tereshkova became one of them. She was the very first woman EVER to go to space. So how did an ordinary Russian do it? Easy. She had learnt to do something extraordinary. And it was this skill that got her noticed. The rest is history.

43

> "A bird cannot fly with one wing only. Human spaceflight cannot develop any further without the active participation of women."
>
> **Valentina Tereshkova**

NAME: **Valentina Vladimirovna Tereshkova**

BORN: **6 March 1937**

NATIONALITY: **Russian**

PROFESSION: **Cosmonaut**

In 1961, the Russians sent the first person into space. He was a man called Yuri Gagarin. Next, they wanted to send the first woman into space too. All they had to do was choose one female cosmonaut from millions of Russian women.

Meanwhile, Valentina Tereshkova had one of the coolest hobbies in the world – parachuting. This just happened to be a super handy way of getting back down to Earth after a spaceflight. So Valentina made it onto the shortlist. After some very tough cosmonaut training, it was finally decided: she would be the one.

On 16 June 1963, Valentina Tereshkova rocketed through Earth's atmosphere on board *Vostok 6* to become the first woman in space. Her parents were astonished – Valentina had told them that she was taking part in a skydiving competition.

"There was never a question in my mind that I wanted to climb that mountain, no matter what other people said."

Junko Tabei

JUNKO TABEI
EXTREME MOUNTAINEER

Junko Tabei was often told that she should be looking after children, not climbing mountains. But she ignored what other people thought and did it anyway. She climbed mountains all over the world, including every continent's highest peak. She also campaigned for sustainable mountaineering. She wanted mountaineers to climb mountains, but she wanted them to look after them too.

NAME: **Junko Tabei**

BORN: **22 September 1939**

DIED: **20 October 2016**

NATIONALITY: **Japanese**

PROFESSION: **Mountaineer**

Junko climbed her first mountain on a school trip. She loved it. But her family couldn't afford to pay for all the equipment she'd need to be a mountaineer. So she gave up on the idea – for now – and trained to be a teacher instead.

When she was older, Junko founded a ladies' climbing club. Together, they tackled Annapurna III in Nepal, which is 7,555 metres high. Four of them – including Junko – made it to the summit. Next, the team decided to climb Everest, which measures 8,848 metres. It's also the highest mountain in the world. They survived an avalanche on the way up, and on 16 May 1975, Junko became the first woman to conquer Everest!

Junko went on to become the first woman to climb the highest peak on each continent. By the age of 69, she had climbed 160 mountains.

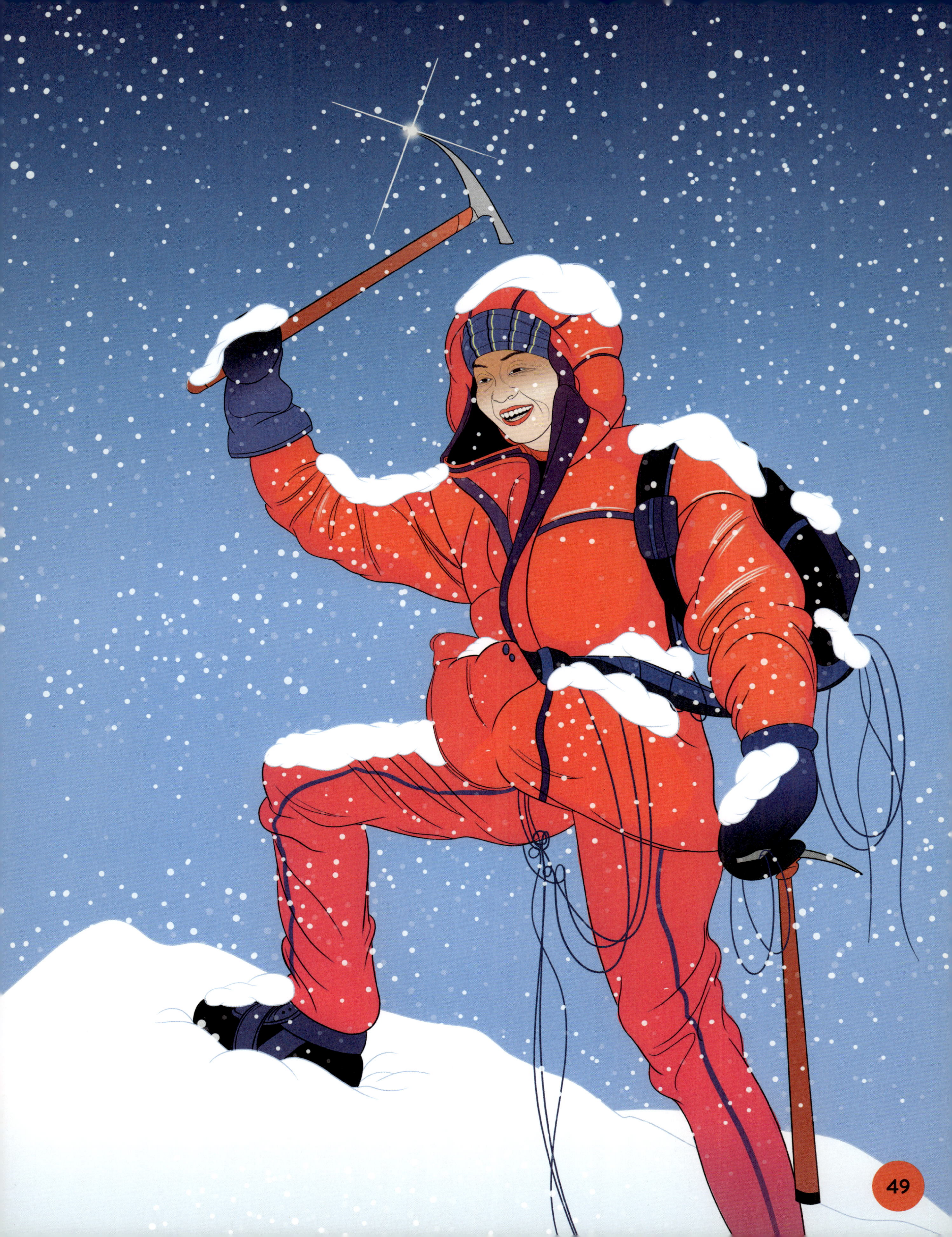

ZAHA HADID
STARCHITECT

Zaha Hadid designed some of the most imaginative buildings and structures ever. Skyscraper? Tick. Exhibition centre? Tick. Aquatics centre, art museum, opera house, bridge, ski jump, car factory and football stadium? Zaha designed them all. She was strong-willed and daring and always brilliant. Her fabulous designs dazzle the world today.

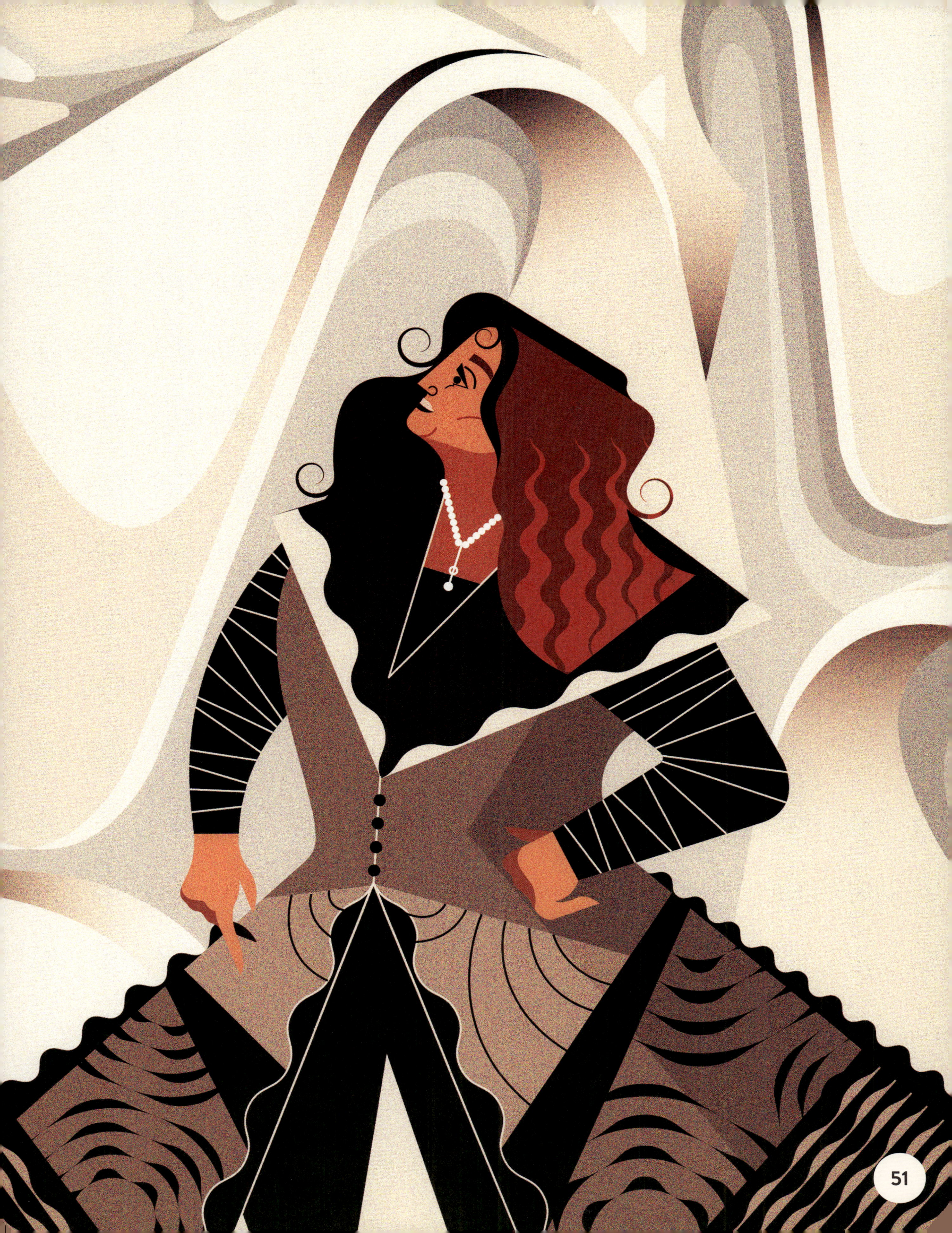

NAME: **Dame Zaha Mohammed Hadid**

BORN: **31 October 1950**

DIED: **31 March 2016**

NATIONALITY: **British and Iraqi**

PROFESSION: **Architect**

Before Zaha Hadid could work as an architect she had to study – a lot. But she worked hard and wowed her professors with her ideas. Next, she taught other architecture students. She also carried on designing. At last, one of her designs was built.

Slowly, Zaha's fame grew. She became known as Queen of the Curve because of the shape of her designs. Just take a look at the London Aquatics Centre, built for the 2012 London Olympics. The Port Authority Building in Antwerp, Belgium looks like something out of a science fiction film. Meanwhile, Zaha said that the Guangzhou Opera House in China was inspired by pebbles in a stream.

In 2004, Zaha became the first woman to win the Pritzker Architecture Prize – the most important architecture prize in the UK. She was made a Dame in 2012.

> "Women are always told, 'You're not going to make it, it's too difficult, you can't do that, don't enter this competition, you'll never win it.' They need confidence in themselves and people around them to help them to get on."

Zaha Hadid

54

MICHELLE OBAMA

GIRLS' CHAMPION

Michelle Obama was born in Chicago, USA, where her childhood was pretty ordinary. She grew up living in an apartment. She went to school down the road. She played Monopoly. There wasn't a limo or a world leader in sight...

NAME: **Michelle LaVaughn Robinson Obama**

BORN: **17 January 1964**

NATIONALITY: **American**

PROFESSION: **Lawyer, campaigner, once the First Lady of the USA**

When Michelle wanted to go to Princeton – one of the USA's top universities – teachers tried to change her mind. She was just a girl. She was setting her sights too high, they said. Michelle went anyway. Then she became a lawyer. She met and later married Barack Obama. He was also a lawyer, but not for long.

In 2008, Barack Obama became the President of the USA. In 2012, he won a second term as president. And for eight years Michelle was the First Lady of the United States. As well as her official duties, she worked hard on projects that she loved. She knew that 62 million girls worldwide did not go to school – she did her best to help them.

She is no longer at the White House. But whatever Michelle does next, she will own it.

"When they go low, we go high."

Michelle Obama

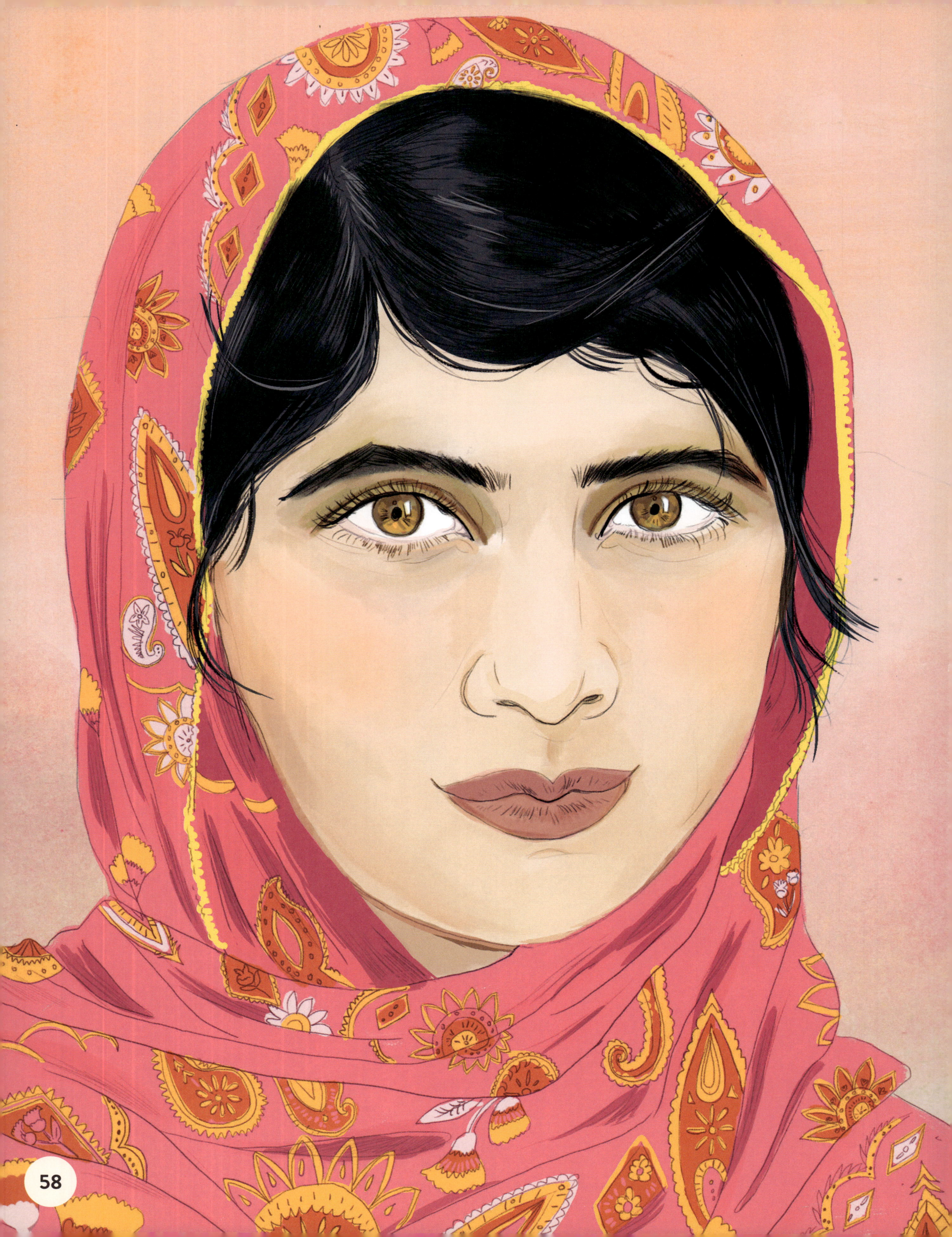

MALALA YOUSAFZAI

FEARLESS ACTIVIST

Malala Yousafzai was just ten years old when the Taliban banned girls from going to school. But she fought back, any way she could. She spoke out against the Taliban on TV and blogged about life under the Taliban's rule. She campaigned for her right to an education. Then Taliban gunmen tried to kill her. They didn't succeed. Malala is still fighting for education.

NAME: **Malala Yousafzai**

BORN: **12 July 1997**

NATIONALITY: **Pakistani**

PROFESSION: **Education activist**

Malala Yousafzai was born in north-western Pakistan. She had always loved to learn. But then an Islamic political group called the Taliban took over the area where she lived. They brought in strict new laws. One law banned girls from going to school. Malala thought the ban was deeply unfair. So she spoke out against the Taliban, any way she could. Two years later, the ban on girls' education was partly lifted.

Malala was awarded the International Children's Peace Prize and Pakistan's National Youth Peace Prize for her brave actions. But she also received death threats, and in 2012 Malala was shot and seriously wounded by Taliban gunmen. She was just 15.

After an incredible recovery, Malala celebrated her sixteenth birthday by giving a speech at the United Nations in New York City, USA. The following year, she became the youngest person ever to be awarded the Nobel Peace Prize.

> *We must believe in the power and strength of our words. Our words can change the world.*

Malala Yousafzai

WONDER WOMEN TIMELINE

1934
Dr Jane Goodall

1913–2005
Rosa Parks

1907–1954
Frida Kahlo

1937
Valentina Tereshkova

1939–2016
Junko Tabei

1950–2016
Zaha Hadid

69 BCE–30 BCE
Cleopatra

1412–1431
Joan of Arc

1815–1852
Ada Lovelace

1897–1937
Amelia Earhart

1867–1934
Marie Curie

1820–1913
Harriet Tubman

1964
Michelle Obama

1997
Malala Yousafzai

TRUE STORIES OF

ICONIC WOMEN

TO INSPIRE A NEW GENERATION

INDEX

A
activists 21, 36, 59, 60
architecture 50–52
art 30–33
aviation 26–29
awards and prizes 22, 24, 52, 60

B
Babbage, Charles 17
Becquerel, Henri 24

C
Caesar, Julius 8
chimpanzee behaviour 38–40
civil rights 21, 34-36
Cleopatra 6–9
communist 30
computer science 14, 17
conservation 38–41
Curie, Marie 22–25
Curie, Pierre 24

D
discrimination 18, 36, 60

E
Earhart, Amelia 26–29
education for girls 15-16, 23–24, 56, 59-60
Egypt 6-9
environmental campaigners 38–41

F
feminism 30, 56, 60

G
Goodall, Dr Jane 38–41
Gagarin, Yuri 45

H
Hadid, Zaha 50–53

J
Jane Goodall Institute 40
Joan of Arc 10–13

K
Kahlo, Frida 30–33

L
Lovelace, Ada 14–17

M
military leaders 10-13
mountaineering 46–49

N
Nobel Prize winners 23, 24, 60

O
Obama, Michelle 54-57

P
Parks, Rosa 34–37
politicians 56, 60
prizes and awards 22, 24, 52, 60

R
racism 18, 21, 35-36

S
science 14-17, 23-24
segregation 35-36, 59-60
slavery 18-21
social media 59-60
space exploration 42–45
sport 45-49

T
Tabei, Junko 46-49
Taliban 59, 60
Tereshkova, Valentina 42–45
Tubman, Harriet 18-21

U
Underground Railroad 21
United Nations speeches 60

W
women's rights 60

Y
Yousafzai, Malala 58-61